I0816794

The blues is a moan. The blues is a shout.
The blues is a boy named Riley B. King.
The blues is a holler.
The blues is a hum.
The blues is lovebirds squawking.
The blues is a goodbye song.

The blues is the Great Depression when jobs were hard to find.
The blues is empty pockets and busted work boots.
The blues is blinding snow with no coat to brave the cold.
The blues is a drowsy sigh with no pillow for your head.

The blues is a wandering child searching for a home.
The blues is a restless dreamer reaching for what he can't see.
The blues is a weeping mother turning on a bed of tears.
The blues is a grieving father suffering great loss in silence.

The blues is black like the midnight sky.
The blues is yellow like morning light.
The blues is a boy. The blues is a girl.
The blues is a voice singing away the blues.

BLUES BOY

The B. B. King Story

BY ALICE FAYE DUNCAN

PAINTINGS BY CARL JOE WILLIAMS

Greenwillow Books
An Imprint of HarperCollinsPublishers

A seed took root and bloomed like a flower in 1925. His parents named him Riley B. King. He was born in a cabin on a farm in Berclair, Mississippi.

Life was a struggle for Riley in the segregated South. Blacks could not dine at public lunch counters or borrow books from the local library. Whites and Blacks lived divided lives.

COLORED

Riley's parents worked as farmers. They separated when he was very young. Then, when Riley was nine, his loving mother died. Before she passed to Glory and earned her angel wings, Mama Nora hugged Riley tightly and spoke these parting words: *When you do good and treat folks right, good things will come to you.*

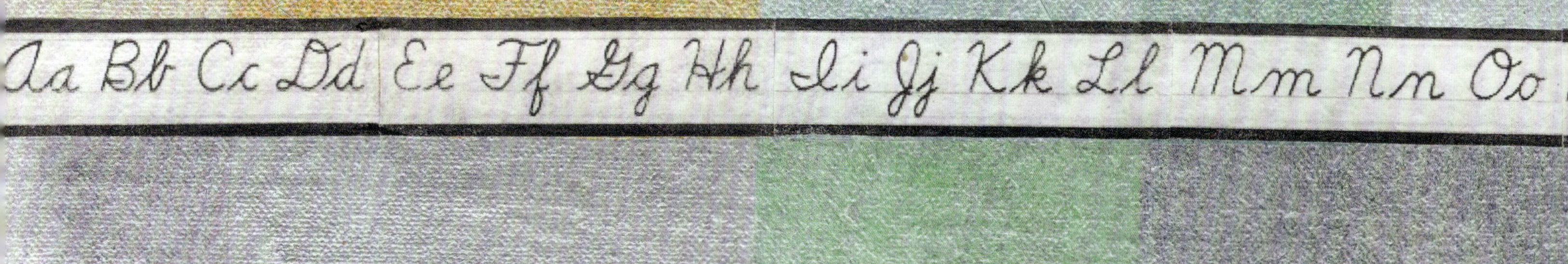

Riley tucked those words in the pocket of his heart and moved to his grandmother's home in Kilmichael, Mississippi. His mother's mother, Granny Farr, sent Riley to the one-room school where he learned to read and write from his teacher, the great Mr. Luther Henson.

Early on Sunday mornings, Granny Farr took Riley to church, where the preacher played an old guitar. Reverend Fair strummed the strings with spirit until he made his guitar shout.

Riley missed his Mama Nora. Tears would flood his eyes. But when he heard that guitar music, joy zipped across his face.

Hard times went down like a bitter pill as Riley grew big and strong. He chopped cotton alongside his grandmother. He plowed fields behind a mule. The other children laughed at Riley in his patched-up overalls. They teased because he stuttered very badly, and words crumbled in his mouth. With all that teasing, Riley prayed for a miracle. He prayed for a change to roll in fast like rushing water and wash away his shame.

One bright morning, Riley visited his favorite aunt, who lived down the road. Aunt Mima loved blues music. When Riley stood at her door, dressed up in a frown, she called through the rusty screen, "I know what you need!"

Aunt Mima cranked her wood Victrola and played some Texas blues. Blind Lemon Jefferson sang, "I am broke and hungry, ragged and dirty too." He groaned like a preacher, but he was no Bible thumper.

Just like the gospel hymns that Riley heard in church, blues singers on the wood Victrola sang lyrics of deep despair. But the slow, sorrowful guitar music rocked Riley in the arms of bliss. And as Blind Lemon's guitar cried, *WAAH-WAAH-WAAH*, Riley clapped his hands and stomped his feet. The blues chased his frown away.

Riley purchased his first guitar when he was twelve years old. Because he was very poor, he borrowed fifteen dollars from the boss man and picked cotton to pay him back. Private guitar lessons cost big money, so Riley did the next best thing. He bought a cheap guitar music book from the Sears Roebuck catalog.

NICK MANOLOFF'S
SPANISH GUITAR METHOD
BOOK
No. 1
THE LATEST, MOST MODERN,
COMPLETE and THOROUGHLY
ILLUSTRATED method ever written
Teaches the most PRACTICAL
FINGERBOARD HARMONY;
Circle of Chords; Chord Relations;
MODERN ORCHESTRA,
RADIO and RECORDING
ACCOMPANIMENT
Published by
M. M. COLE
Publishing Co.
Chicago

Riley commenced to strum the strings. *Dwang! Dwang! Dwang!* The music was clunky at first. His chords were crude and rough. But Riley was no quitter. He practiced in the mornings. He practiced past midnight. After a few years passed? *Dwing! Dwing! Dwing!* Lima beans! He made his guitar rock.

As time rolled on like a river, Riley hoped for better days. He was tired of raggedy britches and busted work boots. He was weary of segregation and Jim Crow signs. How would it feel to be free? How would it feel to be accepted and travel around the world?

Riley wrestled with these questions in his sleep. And when the morning sun appeared, he went to school, studied his books, and helped his grandmother in the fields.

Like King David on his harp, Riley lived for the love of music. He formed a gospel quartet with three other teenage boys and together they became the Elkhorn Jubilee Singers. Their bright voices lifted many souls. In a loud spirit of praise, the worshippers waved their hands, fluttered their fans, and shook their tambourines.

As Riley picked his guitar, power surged through his fingers. When he opened his mouth to sing, his stutter disappeared.

Then one cold day in January, Granny Farr passed away. Grief broke Riley's heart, again. The year was 1940.

With Granny Farr gone to Heaven, Riley lived with his father, stepmother, and their brood of busy children in Lexington, Mississippi. The crowded house did not feel like love and Riley ran away. He rode his bike across ditches and fields with his guitar on his back.

Finally, Riley landed a job in Indianola, Mississippi. It was a tiny Delta town where he drove a huge tractor on the Johnson Barrett farm.

When Riley found a spot to play his blues guitar, life in Indianola turned golden as tupelo honey. Every Saturday night beneath a lamppost on the corner of Church and Second Street, he sang blues serenades, soft, slow, and soulful.

As Riley made his guitar coo, Black men and women dropped shiny coins in his guitar case. *Clink! Clink! Clink!* After long days picking cotton in the blistering sun, they dressed up fine to ease the strain of field work with Riley's feel-good blues.

Come Saturday night, when the sun disappeared and the moon was high, Riley would change his sound to bouncing beats. The good-time people would shift the mood too. They'd cut loose dancing with hips swinging. And like the great Lonnie Johnson from New Orleans, Riley would riff on a single guitar string. His fingers made the guitar speak with a red, burning fever. He'd shout, "HEY-HEY!" And as sweat beaded on the dancers' faces, they'd holler and hoot.

After busking on the corner and collecting loads of coins, Riley would look at the moon and remember his mother's words: *When you do good and treat folks right, good things will come to you.*

Riley had to pick a side. He could plow the cotton fields for a steady paycheck. Or he could play his blues and plant seeds of joy.

Riley chose music. And while the dancing people on Church and Second never left his heart, Riley tipped his hat and departed Indianola. It was time to travel.

In 1948, he hopped on the back of a grocery truck and followed the road until he reached the bright lights of Memphis, Tennessee.

Memphis is famous for Beale Street, where blues music fills the air. Riley played his guitar in Beale Street clubs and took a radio job spinning records at station WDIA.

As his popularity in Memphis grew, Riley purchased an electric guitar from the Houck music store. He named his guitar "Lucille." As for himself, he took the stage name Beale Street Blues Boy, and *BLUES BOY* stuck like glue.

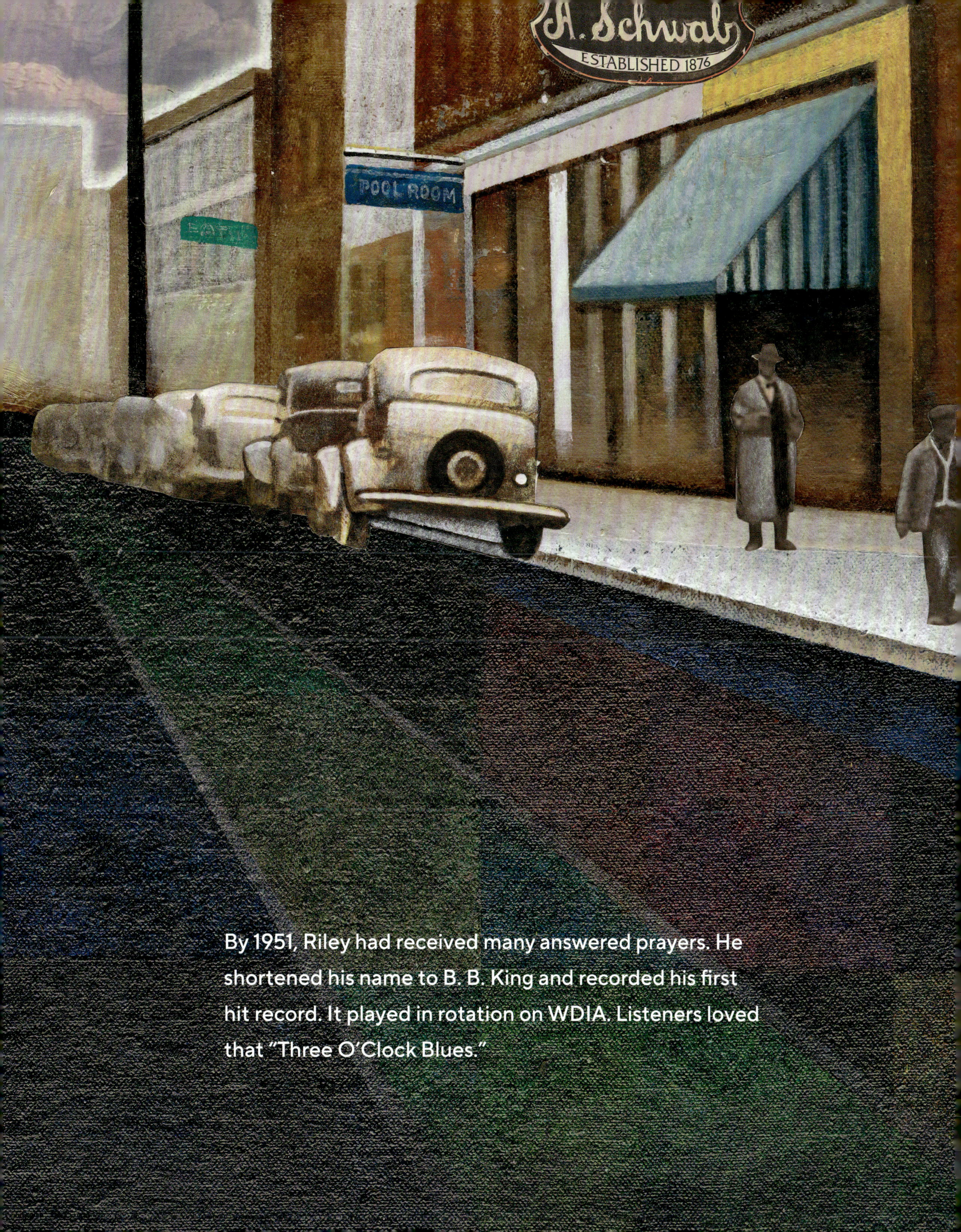

By 1951, Riley had received many answered prayers. He shortened his name to B. B. King and recorded his first hit record. It played in rotation on WDIA. Listeners loved that "Three O'Clock Blues."

With endless nights singing and playing, Riley devoted his life to the blues. Miss Lucille bonded with his soul, the place where music is born. As the "Three O'Clock Blues" climbed the charts, nobody mocked B. B. King. Nobody taunted or teased. The young star bought fancy clothes and formed a large blues orchestra with guitars, horns, and drums.

His orchestra played for Black fans only during the days of segregation. Then in 1964, the civil rights movement marched through America's streets. Legal segregation did not survive. The Jim Crow signs came down.

WDIA
WDIA

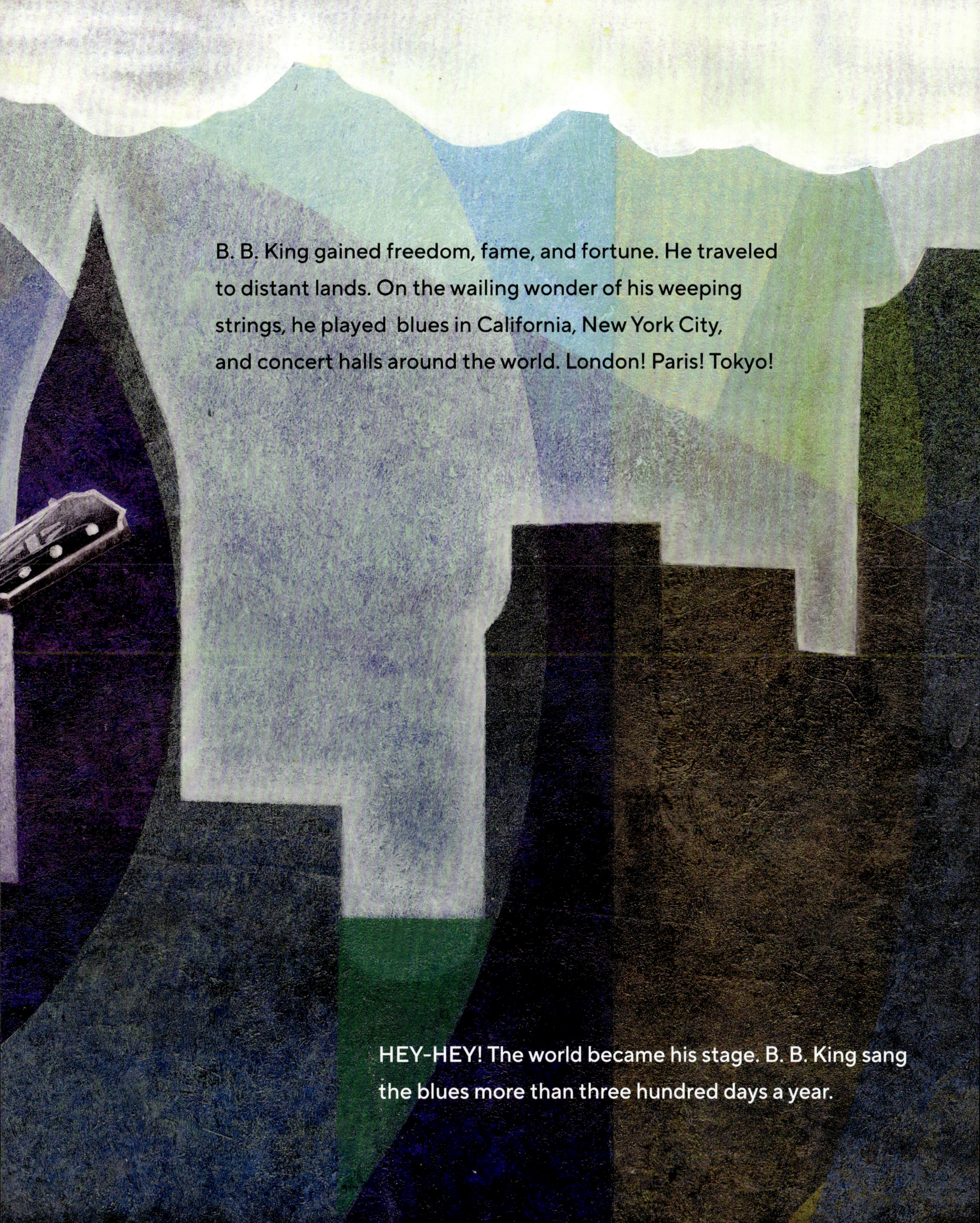

B. B. King gained freedom, fame, and fortune. He traveled to distant lands. On the wailing wonder of his weeping strings, he played blues in California, New York City, and concert halls around the world. London! Paris! Tokyo!

HEY-HEY! The world became his stage. B. B. King sang the blues more than three hundred days a year.

B.B.King

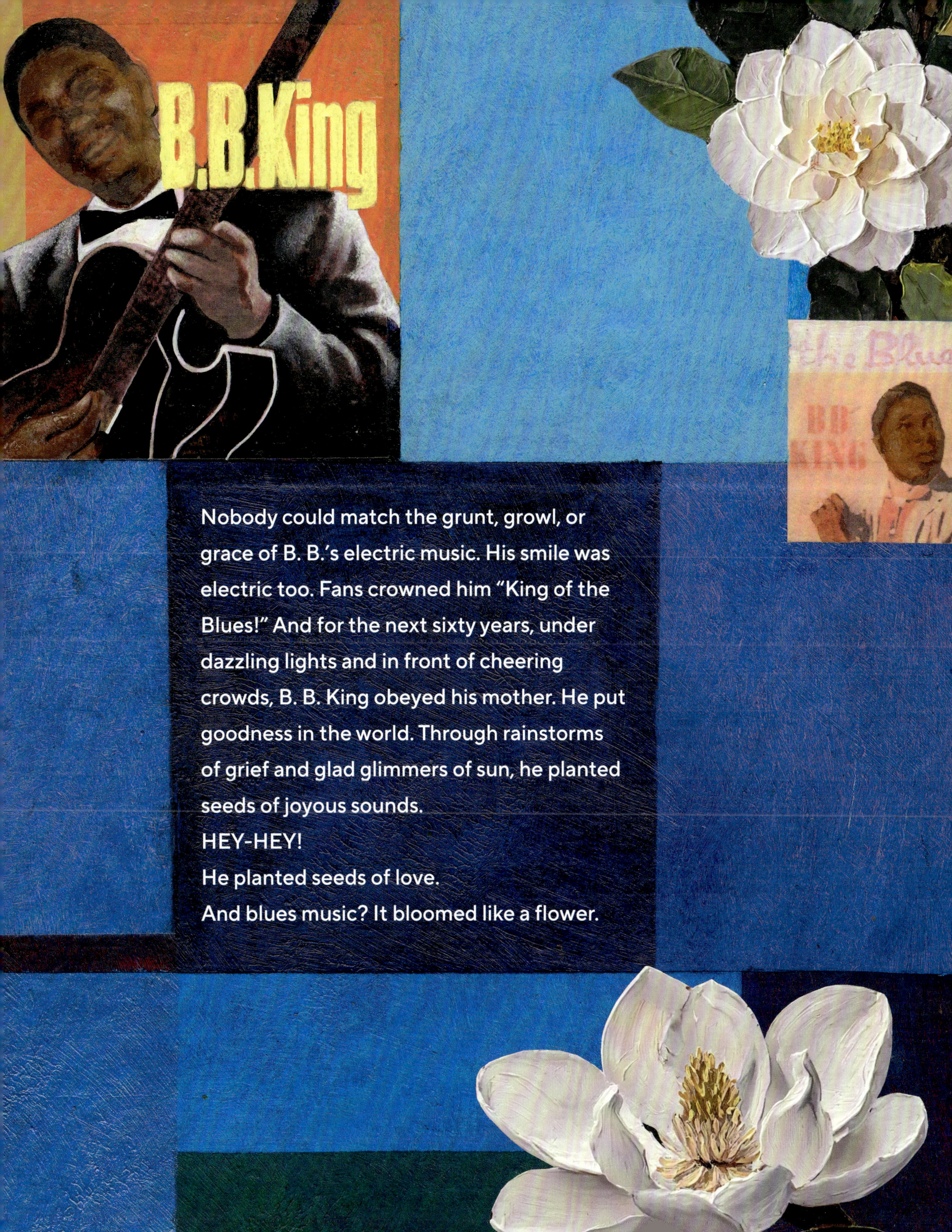

Nobody could match the grunt, growl, or grace of B. B.'s electric music. His smile was electric too. Fans crowned him "King of the Blues!" And for the next sixty years, under dazzling lights and in front of cheering crowds, B. B. King obeyed his mother. He put goodness in the world. Through rainstorms of grief and glad glimmers of sun, he planted seeds of joyous sounds.

HEY-HEY!

He planted seeds of love.

And blues music? It bloomed like a flower.

B. B. King Timeline

1925 ◎ Born in the Mississippi Delta on September 16, 1925. Berclair, Mississippi, is his hometown.

1931–1933 ◎ His parents, Albert and Nora, separate. B. B. King moves to the hills of Kilmichael, Mississippi, with his mother and her maternal relatives.

1935 ◎ His mother dies. Before passing away, she tells B. B. to live right and always "do good."

1936–1940 ◎ Lives with his grandmother Elnora Farr in Kilmichael. B. B. attends the Elkhorn School. He is also a member of the Church of God in Christ (COGIC) and sings with the Elkhorn Jubilee Singers. Pastor Archie Fair is the guitar-playing leader of his church.

1940 ◎ His grandmother dies. B. B. moves to Lexington, Mississippi, with his father.

1941 ◎ Suffering loneliness in his father's house, B. B. King returns to Kilmichael on his bicycle. The 45 miles is a two-day journey.

1942 ◎ Takes shelter and employment with a white farmer, Flake Cartledge.

1943 ◎ Moves to Indianola, Mississippi. B. B. works as a tractor driver. On Saturday nights, he plays his guitar at the corner of Church and Second Street. On Sundays, he sings in church with his second quartet, the St. John Gospel Singers.

1944–1945 ◎ Marries Martha Lee Denton. B. B. is inducted into the US Army but discharged because his skills as a tractor driver are essential to America's economic growth.

1946–1948 ◎ Wrecks a tractor in Indianola. B. B. leaves for Memphis, Tennessee, where he lives with his cousin and music mentor, Bukka White. He returns to Indianola to work and pay his debt for the damaged equipment.

1948–1950 ◎ Moves back to the Memphis area. B. B. works as a disc jockey for the WDIA radio station. He enters a burning club in Arkansas to retrieve his guitar. Afterward, he names his guitar "Lucille." The woman's name is his reminder to live wisely.

1951 ◎ Records his first hit song, "Three O'Clock Blues."

1952 ◎ Signing with the Universal Attractions booking agency, B. B. travels the nation on the Chitlin' Circuit. He gains fame in Black America. He and Martha divorce.

1953 ◎ Leaves his job at WDIA because concert gigs keep him on the road.

1956 ◎ B. B. King and his thriving blues orchestra play 340 one-night engagements.

1958 ◎ His tour bus collides with a butane truck while traveling in Texas. B. B. King is held liable for the damages. The required settlement puts him in debt for several years.

1963 ◎ He records one of his signature songs, "How Blue Can You Get?"

1964 ◎ B. B. King records his famous album *Live at the Regal*. During this Chicago concert, radio personality Pervis Spann is the first to call the musician "King of the Blues."

1968 ◎ Performs at the Fillmore Ballroom in San Francisco, California. It is his first time entertaining an integrated audience. Publicity surrounding the Fillmore concert leads to engagements performing around the world for people of all races, cultures, and nationalities.

1970 ◎ Appears on *The Ed Sullivan Show*. Twenty million Americans watch him perform his famous song "The Thrill Is Gone."

1971 ◎ He travels to London, England, and records a blues album with the Beatles drummer, Ringo Starr.

1984 ◎ Receives induction into the Blues Foundation Hall of Fame.

1987 ◎ Receives induction into the Rock and Roll Hall of Fame and receives a Lifetime Achievement Grammy.

1990 ◎ Receives the National Medal of the Arts.

1995 ◎ Receives the Kennedy Center Honor.

2000 ◎ Records *Riding with the King* with guitarist Eric Clapton. The album sells two million copies and wins the Grammy for Best Traditional Blues Album.

2005 ◎ Governor Haley Barbour declares February 15 is B. B. King day in the state of Mississippi.

2006 ◎ Receives the Presidential Medal of Freedom from President George W. Bush.

2008 ◎ The B. B. King Museum and Delta Interpretive Center opens in Indianola, Mississippi.

2015 ◎ On May 14, B. B. King passes away in Las Vegas, Nevada, of natural causes.

About B. B. King

Hailing from the Mississippi Delta, B. B. King was a singer and blues guitarist who became an international star. Beyond the accolades and shine of fifteen Grammy Awards, he was also inducted into the Blues Foundation Hall of Fame, the Rock and Roll Hall of Fame, and the National Rhythm and Blues Hall of Fame. More than the glitz of fine suits, diamonds, and the spotlight, B. B. King was a humanitarian. During the American civil rights movement, he used his finances to support Dr. Martin Luther King Jr. and the Southern Christian Leadership Conference in efforts to abolish segregation and racial injustice.

At the height of B. B. King's international celebrity in 1970, he visited a large city jail to sing for the prisoners. During his visit, he discovered that the men endured dangerous and unsanitary living conditions. From 1970 until his death in 2015, he used his voice and his music to support prison reform. Specifically, he helped to establish the Foundation for the Advancement of Inmate Rehabilitation and Recreation. With assistance from his band, he also sang free concerts in corrections centers across the nation.

B. B. King was an American music icon who served humanity with love, kindness, and joy. As a tower of dignity and strength, he lived in this way to honor himself, his Mississippi roots, and the memory of his mother, Nora Ella King.

Places to Visit

B. B. King Museum
and Delta Interpretive Center
400 Second Street
Indianola, MS 38751
bbkingmuseum.org

Delta Blues Museum
1 Blues Alley Lane
Clarksdale, Mississippi 38614
deltabluesmuseum.org

Mississippi Civil Rights Museum
222 North Street #2205
Jackson, MS 39201
mcrm.mdah.ms.gov

Discover the Music

B. B. King, *Live at the Regal*, produced by Johnny Pate, recorded November 1964, ABC Records.

B. B. King, *Live in Cook County Jail*, produced by Bill Szymczyk, recorded September 1970, ABC Records.

B. B. King, *Greatest Hits*, a compilation released February 1998 by MCA Records.

B. B. King and Eric Clapton, *Riding with the King*, released June 2000, Duck Records/Reprise.

Suggested Picture Book Readings

Bolden, Tonya, and R. Gregory Christie. *Rock, Rosetta, Rock! Roll, Rosetta, Roll!: Presenting Sister Rosetta Tharpe, the Godmother of Rock & Roll.* HarperCollins, 2023.

Duncan, Alice Faye, and Chris Raschka. *Yellow Dog Blues.* Eerdmans Books for Young Readers, 2022.

Golio, Gary, and E. B. Lewis. *Dark Was the Night: Blind Willie Johnson's Journey to the Stars.* Nancy Paulsen Books, 2020.

Mahin, Michael, and Evan Turk. *Muddy: The Story of Blues Legend Muddy Waters.* Atheneum Books for Young Readers, 2017.

Myers, Walter Dean, and Christopher Myers. *Blues Journey.* Holiday House, 2003.

Bibliography

Alger, Dean. *The Original Guitar Hero and the Power of Music: The Legendary Lonnie Johnson, Music and Civil Rights.* University of North Texas Press, 2014.

Cantor, Louis. *Wheelin' on Beale: How WDIA-Memphis Became the Nation's First All-Black Radio Station and Created the Sound that Changed America.* Pharos Books, 1992.

Conforth, Bruce, and Gayle Dean Wardlow. *Up Jumped the Devil: The Real Life of Robert Johnson.* Chicago Review Press, 2019.

de Visé, Daniel. *King of the Blues: The Rise and Reign of B. B. King.* Grove Press, 2021.

Ferris, William. *Give My Poor Heart Ease: Voices of the Mississippi Blues.* University of North Carolinia Press, 2009.

King, B. B., with David Ritz. *Blues All Around Me: The Autobiography of B. B. King.* It Books, 2011.

King, B. B., with Dick Waterman. *The B. B. King Treasures: Photos, Mementos & Music from B. B. King's Collection.* Bulfinch Press, 2005.

King, Chris Thomas. *The Blues: The Authentic Narrative of My Music and Culture.* Chicago Review Press, 2021.

Mizelle, Richard M., Jr. *Backwater Blues: The Mississippi Flood of 1927 in the African American Imagination.* University of Minnesota Press, 2014.

Sawyer, Charles. *B. B. King: From Indianola to Icon: A Personal Odyssey with the "King of the Blues."* Schiffer Publishing, 2022.

Withers, Ernest C. "I knew B. B. King." American photojournalist remembers taking pictures of B. B. King during his concerts in Memphis, Tennessee. In person interview with the author, May 24, 2006.

Withers, Ernest C., and Daniel J. Wolff. *The Memphis Blues Again: Six Decades of Memphis Music Photographs.* Viking Studio, 2001.

Acknowledgments

Charles Sawyer is a photographer, writer, musician, and blues scholar who documented B. B. King's life for more than forty years. Charles interrupted his own writing to read my draft and advise me on the creation of *Blues Boy*. Thank you, Charlie! Let the good times roll! —A. F. D.

It's been a privilege to work on this book honoring B. B. King. Music has always shaped my art and I try to paint as a way of translating music to visual form, letting rhythm and color spill onto the canvas. Mixing collage with paint lets me layer real life into each piece, creating something new from the familiar. The way an image is built matters deeply to me, and for these illustrations, I blended oils, acrylics, and collage. This book was a long journey, and I'm deeply grateful to everyone who encouraged me along the way. Special thanks to Alice Faye Duncan for her faith in my work, and to Nia Hyatt Eldosougi, Cassandra Payne, and Johnathan Hodge for their support. —C. J. W.

**For Mark Stansbury Sr.—historian,
WDIA radio personality, & friend —A. F. D.**

For my mom, Annie Williams —C. J. W.

HarperCollins Children's Books, a division of HarperCollins Publishers, 195 Broadway, New York, NY 10007

HarperCollins Publishers, Macken House, 39/40 Mayor Street Upper, Dublin 1, D01 C9W8, Ireland

Greenwillow Books is an imprint of HarperCollins Publishers.

Blues Boy: The B. B. King Story

Library of Congress Cataloging-in-Publication Data

Names: Duncan, Alice Faye, author. | Williams, Carl Joe, illustrator.
Title: Blues boy : the B. B. King story / by Alice Faye Duncan ; paintings by Carl Joe Williams.
Description: First edition. | New York : Greenwillow Books, an Imprint of HarperCollins Publishers, 2026. | Includes bibliographical references | Summary: "The aspirational story of American musician B. B. King, from his childhood in the Jim Crow South to his triumphant reign as the King of Blues"— Provided by publisher.
Identifiers: LCCN 2025012962 | ISBN 9780063334021 (hardcover)
Subjects: LCSH: King, B. B.—Juvenile literature. | Blues musicians—United States—Biography—Juvenile literature. | Guitarists—United States—Biography–Juvenile literature. | LCGFT: Biographies.
Classification: LCC ML3930.K46 D86 2026 | DDC 782.421643092 [B]—dc23/eng/20250325
LC record available at https://lccn.loc.gov/2025012962

The artist used oils, acrylics, and collage on paper to create the illustrations for this book.
The text of this book is set in TT Norms Pro Var Roman. Book design by Sylvie Le Floc'h.
25 26 27 28 29 RTLO 10 9 8 7 6 5 4 3 2 1
First Edition

Greenwillow Books